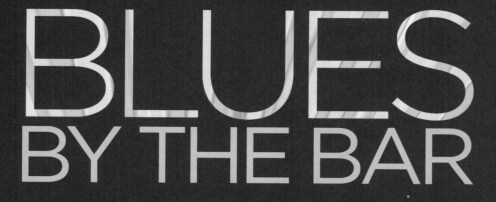

BLUES
BY THE BAR

MASTER CLASS WITH BUZZ FEITEN

Cool Riffs That Sound Great over
Each Portion of the Blues Progression

BY BUZZ FEITEN WITH TOBY WINE

ISBN 978-1-60378-262-3

Visit our website at www.cherrylaneprint.com

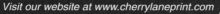

Contents

Introduction

Buzz Feiten knows the blues. This world-renowned musician is a guitarist's guitarist whose work in the studio has graced countless records by great pop and jazz artists. Now Buzz shares his love for and knowledge of the blues with you by taking you through the 12-bar blues chorus step by step, offering a host of authentic licks and phrases to use over each portion of the form. With a wide variety of two-bar examples, covering fast and slow blues in E and C, as well as "stop-time" licks for use on fast breaks, *Blues by the Bar: Master Class* will give you the tools you need to build a formidable blues guitar arsenal.

TRACK 01

Note: Track 1 contains tuning pitches.

About the Authors

—*Buzz Feiten*

Buzz Feiten began his professional career in his teens playing with the Paul Butterfield Blues Band, and appeared with them at Woodstock. His natural gifts as a rhythm guitar player and as a passionate and melodic soloist have led him to record and perform with the likes of Stevie Wonder, Aretha Franklin, the Rascals, Gregg Allman, Bob Dylan, Rickie Lee Jones, Dave Sanborn, and Dave Weckl. He is the inventor of the Buzz Feiten Tuning System.

—Toby Wine

Toby Wine is a native New Yorker and a freelance guitarist, composer, arranger, and educator. He is a graduate of the Manhattan School of Music, where he studied composition with Manny Albam and Edward Green. Toby has performed with Philip Harper (of the Harper Brothers and Art Blakey's Jazz Messengers), Bob Mover, Ari Ambrose, Michael and Carolyn Leonhart (both of Steely Dan), Peter Hartmann, Ian Hendrickson-Smith (of Sharon Jones and the Dap-Kings), Melee, Saycon (currently starring in *Fela!* on Broadway), Nakia Henry, and the Harlem-based rock band Kojomodibo Sun, among others. His arrangements and compositions can be heard on recordings by Tobias Gebb and Unit Seven (*Free at Last,* Yummyhouse Records), Phillip Harper (*Soulful Sin, The Thirteenth Moon*, Muse Records), Ari Ambrose (*Early Song*, Steeplechase), and Ian Hendrickson-Smith (*Up in Smoke*, Sharp Nine). Toby leads his own trio and septet, does studio sessions, and works as a sideman with a variety of tri-state area bandleaders. He spent four years as the music librarian for the Carnegie Hall Jazz band and is currently an instructor at the Church Street School for Music and Art in Tribeca. He is the author of numerous Cherry Lane publications, including *1001 Blues Licks*, *The Art of Texas Blues, 150 Cool Jazz Licks in Tab, Steely Dan: Legendary Licks*, and *Cool Pedal Steel Licks for Guitar.*

About the Audio

When you study the blues several bars at a time, you may lose track of how those two-bar licks fit within the context of a full blues form. Because of this, the licks within this book are compiled into twelve complete solos on the accompanying CD so that you can hear each lick within the context of a complete solo. As you study the notation and tablature for each lick, simply play the noted track number on your accompanying CD to hear the lick on its own, then cue up the full-solo version noted next to it to hear the lick in the context of a complete solo.

The Blues Chorus and Substitutions

Before we can get started on the good stuff—the licks themselves—we need to do a little background work on the basic theory behind the blues. (Note: What follows is aimed at theory geeks. If you want to start playing right away, skip to page 12 and dig in.) Chords and chord progressions are often labeled with Roman numerals for purposes of discussion or analysis; hence, the familiar I-IV-V progression. Essentially, each step of the major scale is given a numeral and has an appropriate chord "quality" (major, minor, diminished, etc.). In the key of C, I is C major, IV is F major, and V is G major, while ii, iii and iv are D minor, E minor, and A minor, respectively. The vii chord is a diminished chord, in this case Bdim. (Note that the minor and diminished chords are given lower-case Roman numerals.) An analysis of a standard 12-bar blues in E would look something like this, keeping in mind that the "qualities" of the chords in a blues progression are normally dominant 7ths, rather than majors:

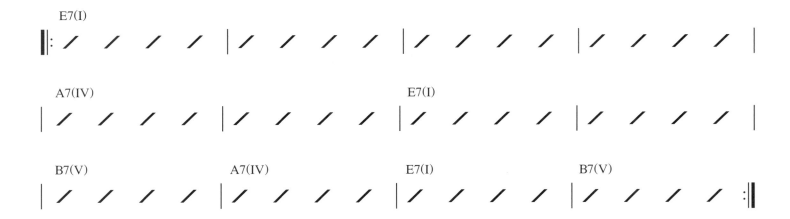

The same progression in the key of C would look like this:

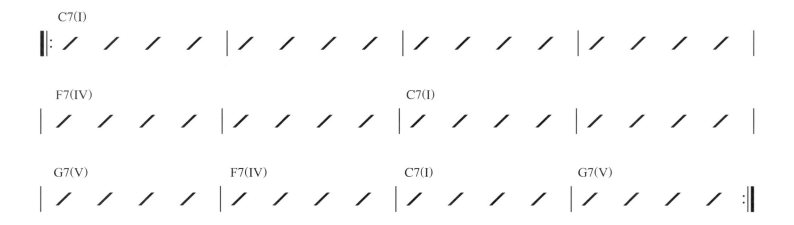

Okay so far? That should look familiar to even beginner players, as it's easily the most commonly encountered chord progression in American music. One common wrinkle added to this basic progression is the "fast IV" in which we shift to the IV chord (A in the key of E, F in the key of C) in measure 2 before returning to the I chord in measures 3 and 4. The fast IV is simply a way of creating a little harmonic interest and breaks up what would be four straight measures of a single chord. Buzz includes the fast IV in both his "fast blues" in the key of E and "slow blues" in the key of C.

The fast IV is one of dozens of possible substitutions used in the blues. The various styles and sub-genres in which blues progressions are played each have their own favored substitutions, so the basic chords may be augmented by any number of additions depending on whether you're playing with rock, jazz, country, or gospel musicians. Tempo can also be an important arbiter when it comes to chord substitutions; in general, the faster the blues, the simpler the chords. A slow blues leaves the band with a lot more time to fill and the opportunity to add a wide variety of substitutions, as Buzz does in his Slow Blues section of this book. Working in the key of C, Buzz solos over the following progression, once more shown below with Roman numerals next to the chord symbols for analytical purposes:

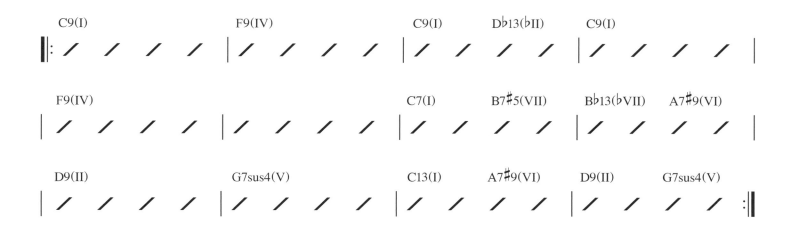

There's a lot going on here, so let's take it a step at a time. First, any *dominant* chord (that is, a dominant 7th–type chord, having a major 3rd and flatted 7th) can be adorned with various chord extensions, as shown by, for example, the I (C9 and, later, C13). The 9th and 13th are present in both the major pentatonic scale (C-D-E-G-A in the key of C) and in the Mixolydian mode, the most natural fit for a dominant 7th chord (have a friend play a C7 chord while you run through the notes of the C Mixolydian mode and you'll hear just how smoothly these notes blend with the chord; it's not exactly the sound of rock and blues guitar but it works nicely and can be a refreshing addition to a steady diet of pentatonic licks). This mode is essentially a major scale with a flatted 7th degree. (A C Mixolydian mode would be C-D-E-F-G-A-B♭, while an F Mixolydian mode is F-G-A-B♭-C-D-E♭.) The 9th extension is synonymous with the major 2nd but is played an octave higher, going past the tonic (the 8th scale step), while the 13th is synonymous with the 6th in the higher octave. In relation to a C dominant chord the 9th would be an added D while the 13th would be an added A in the upper register. These "unaltered" extensions are used freely to add color to a dominant chord throughout the blues progression and in many other contexts. The descending progression in measures 7 and 8 feature B and A dominant chords adorned with "altered" extensions (B7♯5 and A7♯9) which create added tension but also retain a smooth sound, as the extensions remain firmly in the key of C. The ♯5 on the B chord is a G (the 5th of C) and the ♯9 on the A chord is a C (the tonic of the song), so no feathers are ruffled, while the B♭13 chord passes between them chromatically and also features an extension (the 13th, G) that stays in the key. It is beyond the scope of this book to fully explain the many ways to apply chord extensions, but suffice it to say that if you keep the I and IV chords in an "unaltered" condition, you'll be safe. (Try playing the blues beginning with C7♯5 and F7♯5 chords and you'll see just how jarring the altered extensions can be when used "incorrectly.") This isn't to say that it can't be done, or that they can't be used in precisely this way, but it takes a special set of circumstances and a specific desire to hear these altered sounds in order to justify their use.

Let's move on. In measure 3, after returning from the "fast IV," we encounter both the I (C9) and ♭II (D♭9) chords. In this case, the D♭9 chord should be considered a chromatic passing chord—moving up a half step and then back down to C9 in measure 4—and is another tool employed to create a sense of motion, tension, and overall interest in the background over which Buzz is soloing. The D♭9 chord can also be heard in the pickup to the blues chorus, before the downbeat of measure 1. Once again, it's being used as a passing chord and has no true harmonic function in this context; Buzz doesn't move his licks up into the key of D♭ to address it specifically. Instead, he stays with his C soloing ideas and lets a bit of tension build up beneath him before it's resolved with the shift back down to C9. The descending sequence in measures 7 and 8 also serve a similar purpose, creating a chromatic bridge between the I chord and VI chord (A7♯9). In a basic harmonic context, the vi would be an A minor chord (not a dominant VI), but the exchange of minor to dominant is a very common practice here (and in many other styles). The altered VI dominant chord gives the progression a jazzy sound, creating a tension that releases as it moves up to the following D9 chord. The B7♯5 and B♭13 chords preceding the A7♯9 serve as chromatic connectors and have little true harmonic function in the sense that Buzz doesn't solo over each with its own scale, instead staying with licks in the key of C as they move beneath him. In a true jazz setting the soloist would be much more likely to address each of these chords with its own scale or mode but the pure blues vibe would most likely be lost in the process.

Now let's take a look at the last four measures. In analysis, we see that there is a full measure each of the II and V chords, followed by a I-VI-II-V progression in which each chord lasts for two beats. Both the II-V and I-VI-II-V progressions are extremely common in a variety of styles. The II in this case is a D9 chord, rather than the D minor chord that might be encountered in a simpler song, and the transformation to a dominant chord serves a similar purpose to the A7♯9 chord that precedes it—namely, to build tension as it moves up to the G7sus4 chord that follows. This suspended sound simply smoothes out the progression, as the added 4th interval is a C, the tonic of the song. The final two-measure turnaround accelerates the process found within the preceding measures, moving from I (C13) to VI (A7♯9) to the same II (D9) and V (G7sus4) chords previously encountered. Play through the progression carefully and check out just how sweet these substitutions sound. Try adding them to your blues work as you go forward, and examine both transcriptions and recordings of your favorite blues songs to see where else they are used and what other types of substitutions you run across. The possibilities are nearly endless.

Scales and Modes
for Blues Soloing

Before we move on to the licks, there's one other topic we need to cover—the scales and modes Buzz uses to create his ideas. While there are as many options for single-note playing as there are for chord substitutions and comping, Buzz, and the majority of blues soloists in general, draws from three primary sources: the minor pentatonic scale, the major pentatonic scale, and the afore-mentioned Mixolydian mode. The minor pentatonic scale is at the core of blues and rock soloing and should be familiar to nearly all readers. The scale is shown below in both E and C, starting on the low E (6th) string at the 12th and 8th frets, respectively.

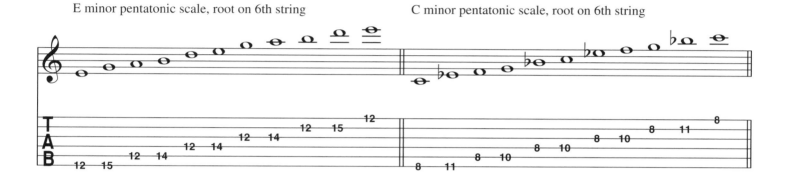

You may already know these patterns, but do you know how to play the same scales begin-ning on the A string? Having at least two ways of playing a given scale is essential, as all the great soloists—Buzz included—shift and slide their way between multiple fingering positions constantly. Check out the fingerings for the E- and C-minor pentatonic scales beginning on the A (5th) string:

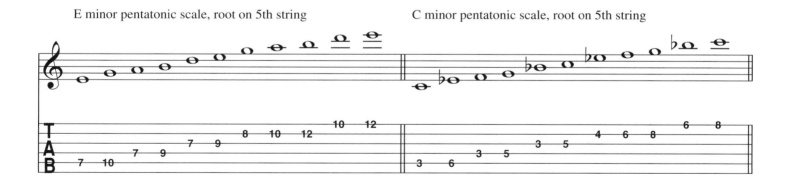

Whenever there are three notes on a single string, with each note two frets apart (as on the B string in the previous example), be sure to use your index, middle, and pinky fingers; skip the ring finger in this situation.

The second most common scale used for blues soloing is the major pentatonic scale. It is the great dichotomy of the blues that both major and minor sounds can coexist in a single measure and over a single chord. Unlike the minor pentatonic scale, however, the major pentatonic scale can be affixed to each new chord separately—an E major pentatonic scale would be played over an E7 chord, an A major pentatonic scale would be played over an A7 chord, and a B major pentatonic scale would be played over the B7 chord. The diagram below shows the scale in both E and C, starting on the low E (6th) string. Begin each with your middle finger.

E major pentatonic scale, root on 6th string   C major pentatonic scale, root on 6th string

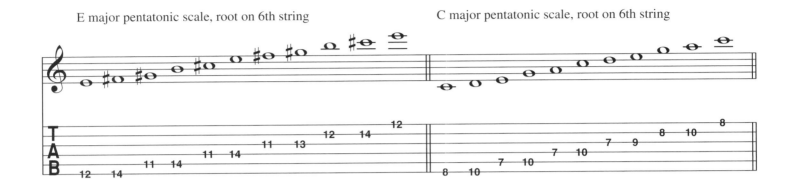

The next diagram shows the same scales beginning on the A (5th) string. Once again, use your index, middle, and ring fingers for the A-string notes. Alternatively, you may want to slide your index finger from the first note to the second, which will put you in good position to finish the scale without further shifting.

E major pentatonic scale, root on 5th string   C major pentatonic scale, root on 5th string

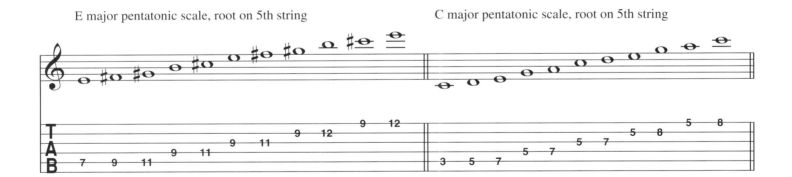

Finally, the Mixolydian mode can be used in the same way as the major pentatonic scale—applied to each chord individually. The E Mixolydian mode would be played over the E7 chord, the A Mixolydian mode fits the A7 chord, and so on. As mentioned earlier, the Mixolydian mode is the truest natural match for a dominant chord, as it contains all the chord tones (1, 3, 5, and ♭7) and the other scale tones that fit smoothly against it (2, 4, and 6, or 9, 11, and 13 in the upper octave). Here is the Mixolydian mode in both E and C beginning on the low E (6th) string:

E Mixolydian mode, root on 6th string

C Mixolydian mode, root on 6th string

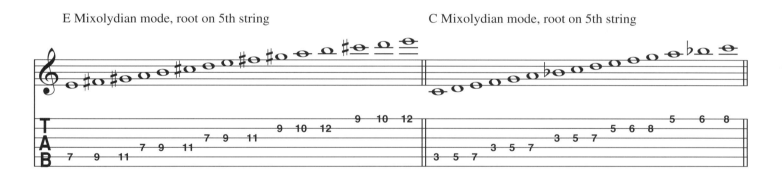

The final diagram shows the same two Mixolydian modes beginning on the A (5th) string:

E Mixolydian mode, root on 5th string

C Mixolydian mode, root on 5th string

As you work your way through this book, take note of what scale or mode Buzz is using during each example. Pay particular attention to the way he combines two or even all three in a single phrase and how he shifts positions to move between the various fingerings of each. Notice that he sometimes employs open-string fingerings for the pentatonic scales—a practice that dates back to the very beginnings of blues in the Mississippi Delta. Don't be content to simply pick up your axe and fly through the licks that follow. Take an analytical stance and unearth the hidden moves behind them. Even the most visceral and primitive blues styles have a logical harmonic and melodic structure at their core, and an in-depth examination reveals unseen complexities that can profoundly affect your playing and understanding of the music. Now let's get to it!

Fast Blues Licks in E

Bars 1 and 2

Let's get started with some great licks for the first two bars of the blues. All the licks in this chapter are in the key of E and work over medium- and up-tempo grooves, although you may also choose to play them in any other context. Notice the variety of positions Buzz employs, from the standard 12th-fret "blues box" in the E minor pentatonic scale, to higher register playing up at the 17th fret, and ninth-position playing below. Be sure to take your favorites here and throughout the book and transpose them to other keys. This will allow you to access them whenever the mood strikes you, regardless of the key or context.

TRACK 02

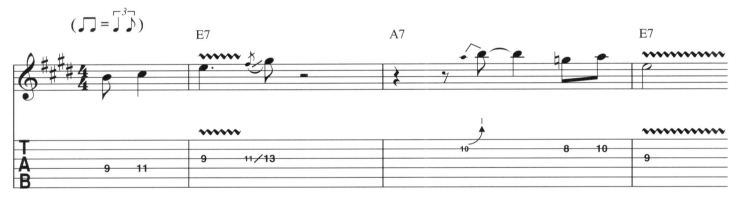

TRACK 03

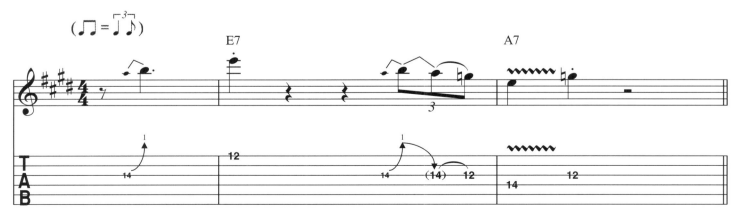

TRACK 04

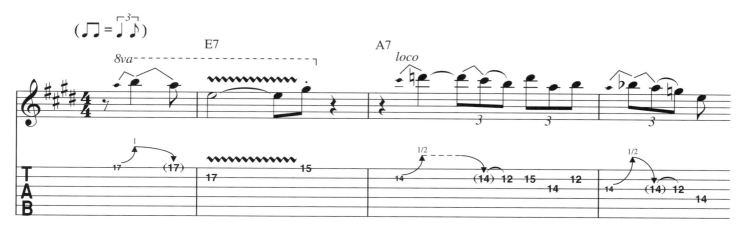

TRACK 05

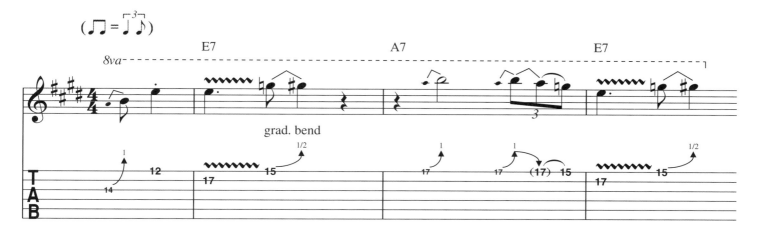

TRACK 06

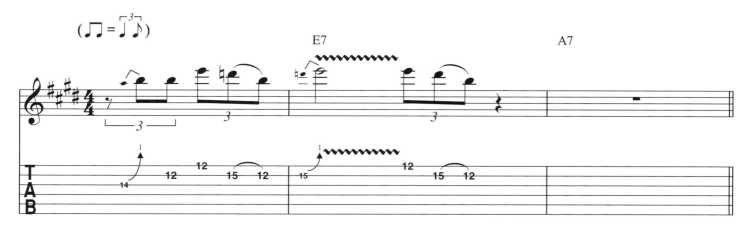

Bars 3 and 4

This segment of the blues chorus features a return to the tonic chord (E7) after the "fast IV" progression. The band sits on the E7 chord for two bars, gearing up for the push to the A7 chord in measure 5. This is a great spot to start building up tension and momentum towards that big harmonic shift around the corner. Buzz once again varies the position of his licks and includes two choice open-string phrases to get us started.

TRACK 09

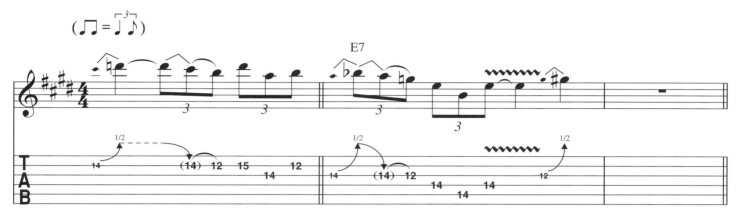

TRACK 10

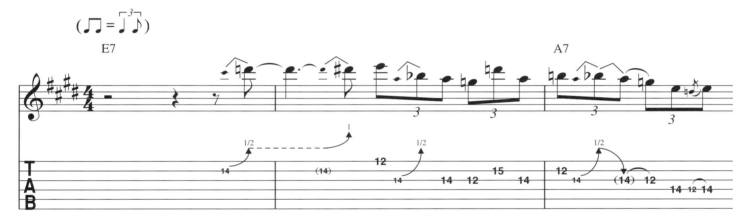

TRACK 11

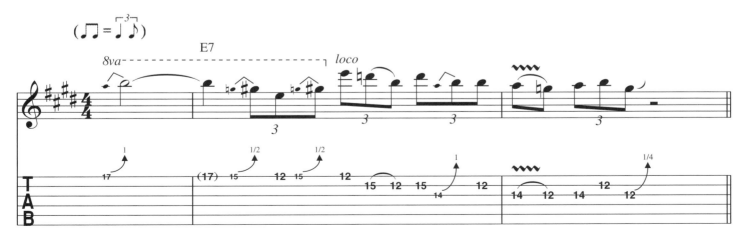

Bars 5 and 6

At this point, we arrive at the IV chord (A7), where we'll remain for two full measures. You have a choice at this juncture—stick with the E minor pentatonic scale, or address the new chord with its own scale (A major pentatonic) or mode (A Mixolydian). Buzz gives us a bit of each approach in the licks that follow, outlining the A7 chord in the first lick and in the pickup to the third lick, using repetition in the second example, staying strictly with classic E minor pentatonic phrasing in the fourth, and mixing it with A major pentatonic tones in the final lick.

TRACK 14

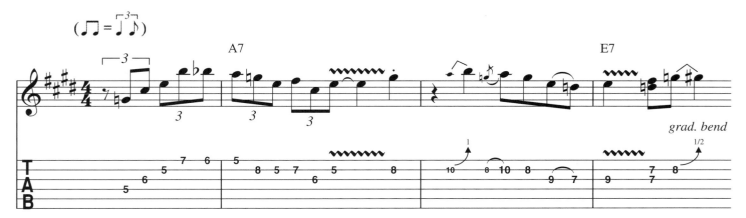

TRACK 15

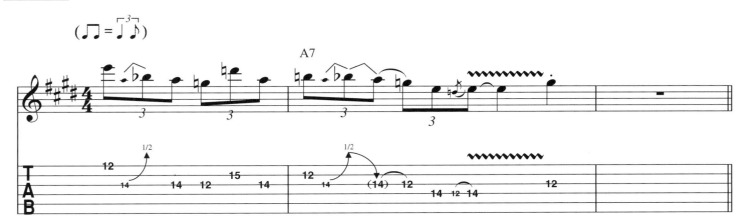

TRACK 16

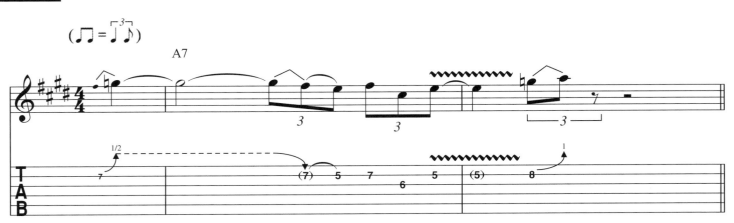

Bars 7 and 8

At this point, we return once again to the tonic chord (E7), staying in a holding pattern for two bars until we make the big move to the V chord in measure 9. This is another spot to build up some momentum for that critical harmonic shift. Note that simply resting or playing a short or uncomplicated phrase here may be extremely effective in building tension. A fast or busy lick isn't always the answer. Buzz demonstrates this approach clearly in the following five examples, using longer rests and shorter phrases that, placed in the context of the 12-bar chorus, will allow the solo to "breathe" and unfold naturally and musically. The last two licks are a bit denser than the earlier phrases, but still end with prominent rests.

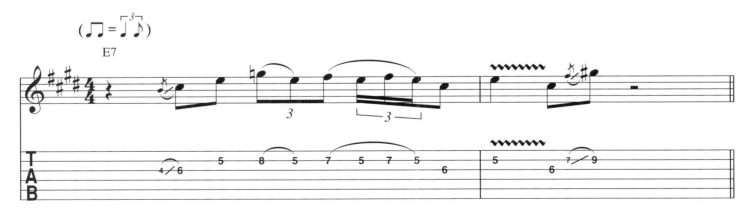

TRACK 19

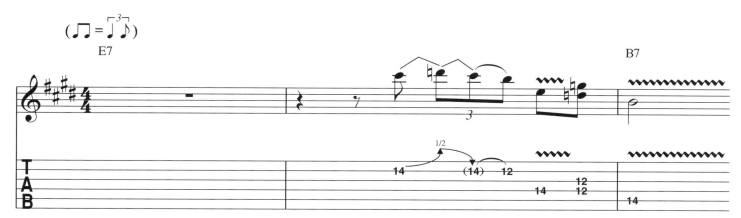

TRACK 20

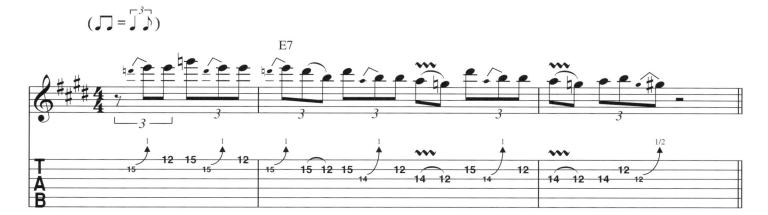

TRACK 21

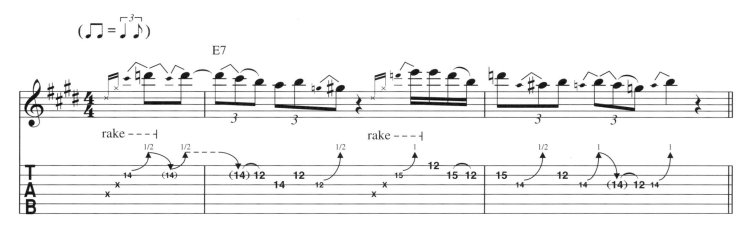

Bars 9 and 10

The blues form builds momentum towards this spot, where we see the V (B7) chord for the first time and start the turnaround towards the end of the chorus. This is when many soloists turn on the gas, bringing out their best tricks and licks to release against the new harmonic background. Buzz demonstrates five of his favorites, including a busy triplet phrase that mixes B minor pentatonic tones with open-position ideas played over A7, some slower developing examples that use rests to great effect, and an intriguing harmonic anticipation in the third lick, where he outlines the A7 chord tones a beat before the band actually arrives on the chord.

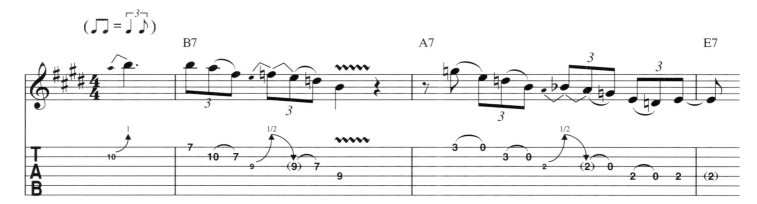

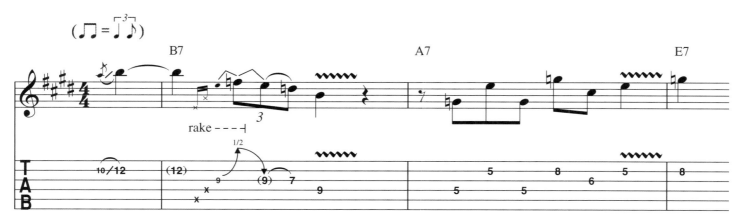

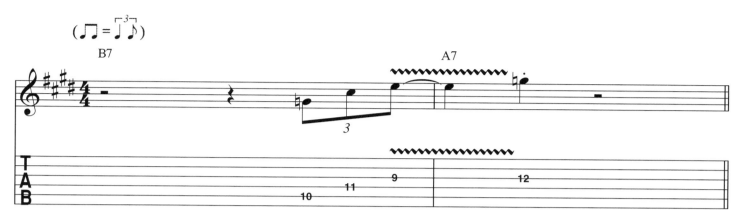

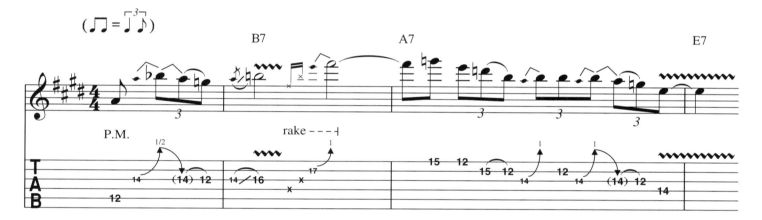

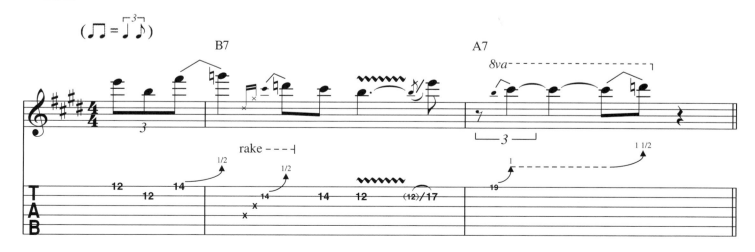

Bars 11 and 12

The final two bars of the blues are often called the "turnaround" and may feature a variety of different chord sequences, or—in this case—a simple return to the I chord (E7). Buzz offers a range of approaches to this section, starting with an open-position pentatonic phrase that descends to the V (B) in classic fashion, even if the band doesn't follow him down to a B7 chord as is often the case here. The fourth lick is an especially tasty example of the familiar descending chord sequence often heard in blues turnarounds and requires you to pluck the lower notes on the D string with the pick while using your fingers to grab the notes on the top two strings.

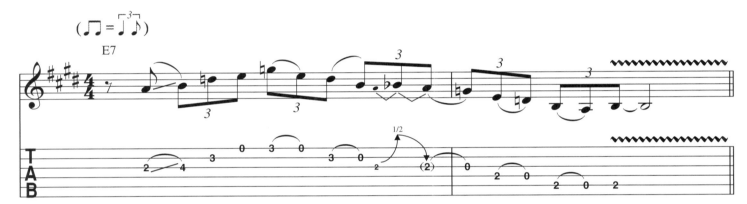

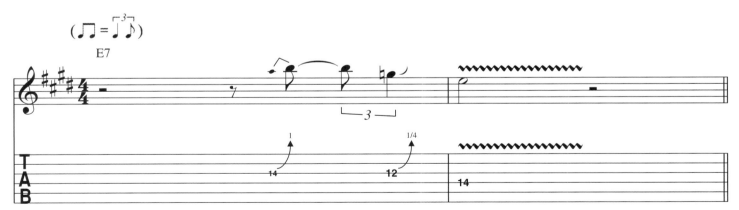

TRACK 29

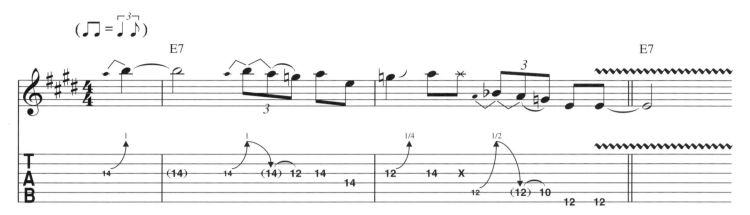

TRACK 30

TRACK 31

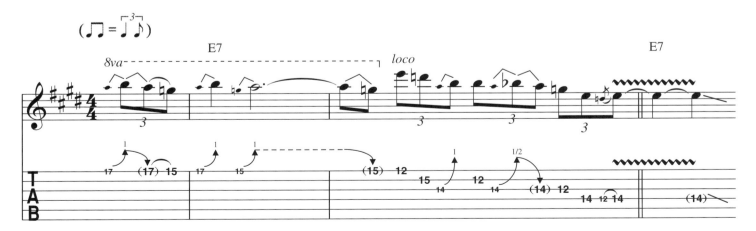

Slow Blues Licks in C

Bars 1 and 2

Contrary to what many musicians believe, slower tempos are often harder to solo over than faster ones, for a variety of reasons. First and foremost, the added time in each measure creates numerous rhythmic and melodic opportunities that simply aren't there when playing at a quicker pace. There is also the stark fact that the additional room in every measure may reveal the soloist's lack of any real musicality! A technically gifted player without a sense of melody or "storytelling" ability will create solos bereft of emotional punch—an essential feature of authentic blues improvisation. The blues is primarily a music of sadness, joy, vulnerability, pain, defiance, and what-have-you; the technical achievements of its best practitioners are usually secondary in importance to their ability to take the listener on an emotional journey while they tell their story. In the following licks, Buzz does just that, giving you a handful of phrases that are musical, rhythmic, and full of emotion. The bends, slides, and vibrato mimic the cry of the human voice in the same manner that has been employed since the birth of the blues.

As we are in a new key and at a slower tempo, take your time to carefully analyze the positional shifts and rhythmic intricacies in this section. Notice that we are now in a 12/8 time signature as well (which has 12 eighth notes per measure). This is really just a very slow 4/4 tempo with three notes (an eighth-note triplet) played or implied per beat.

TRACK 32

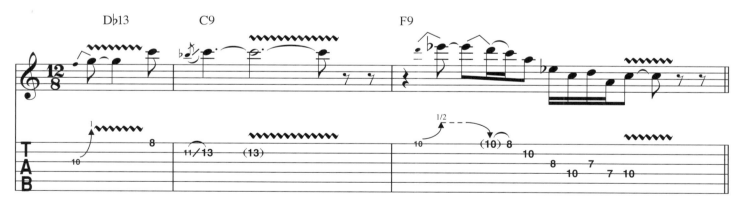

TRACK 33

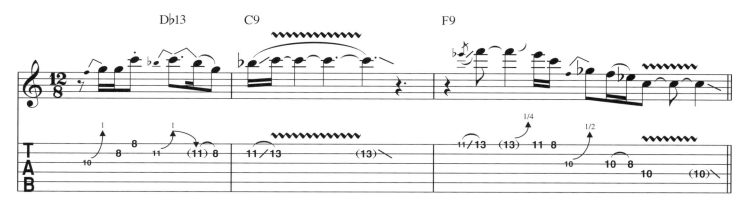

TRACK 34

TRACK 35

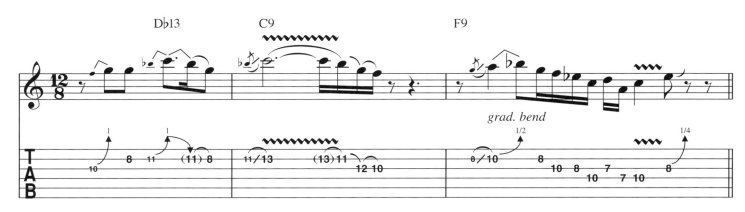

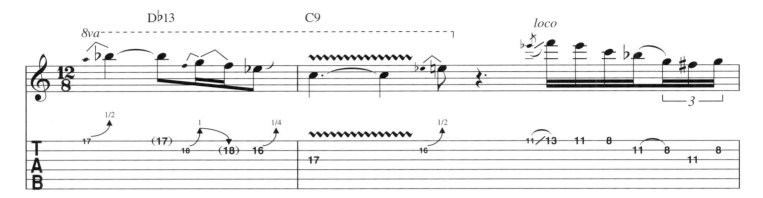

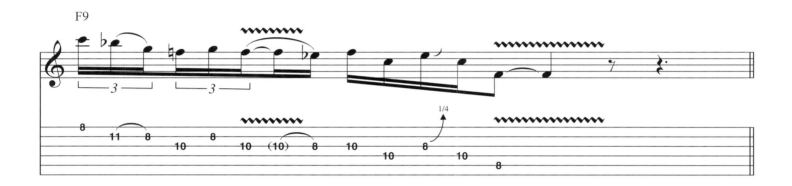

Bars 3 and 4

In the next two-bar segment, the band augments the chord progression with the addition of a Db13 chord, which Buzz chooses not to address directly, instead sticking with his C minor pentatonic phrases in each lick. However, the Eb, F, G, and Bb tones in this scale all match fairly well with the Db13 chord. The F is the major 3rd, while the Eb, G, and Bb represent the 9th, raised 11th, and 13th. These extensions, particularly the raised 11th, give the Db chord a fairly jazzy sound while still retaining the essential blues character of each lick. However, the thinking here is strictly pentatonic—the blending of scale notes with the Db chord is more a happy accident than anything else, although you can be sure Buzz knows exactly what's taking place!

TRACK 37

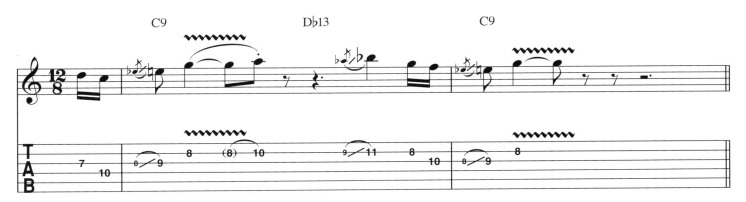

TRACK 38

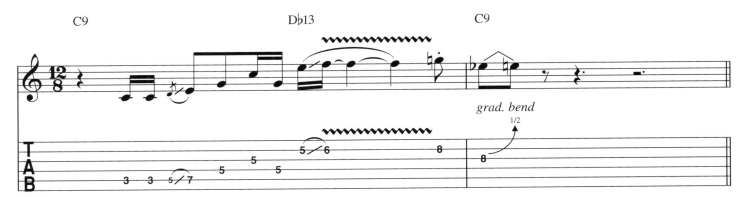

TRACK 39

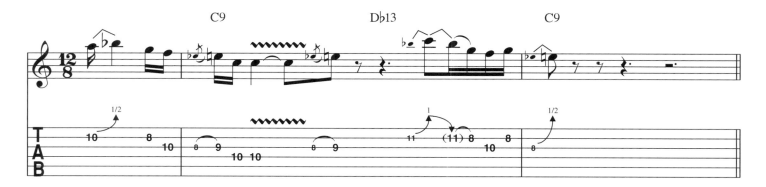

TRACK 40

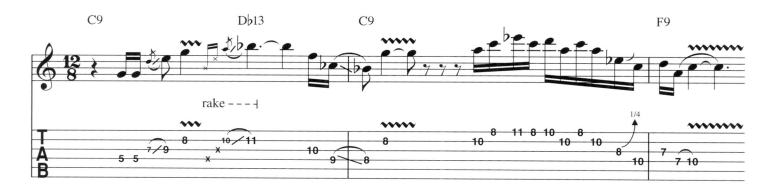

TRACK 41

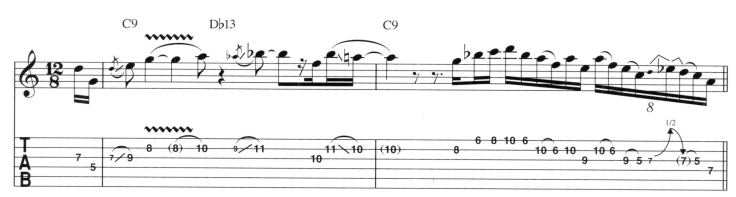

Bars 5 and 6

As we shift to the IV chord (F9) in the following examples, Buzz stays primarily with the C minor pentatonic scale, often augmenting it with the flatted fifth (G♭). The addition of this note turns the pentatonic into a six-note scale most often referred to as the "blues scale." Take note of the brief instances in which Feiten adds notes from the F major pentatonic scale as well; these small additions help to give character to the line while acknowledging the change in the underlying harmony. A few A or D notes here and there go a long way towards creating an authentic blues sound and pull the player out of what can often become a bit of a trap within the minor pentatonic or blues scales.

TRACK 42

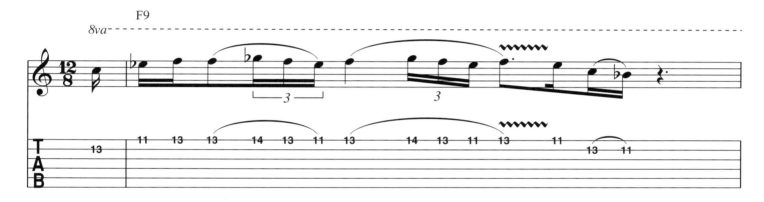

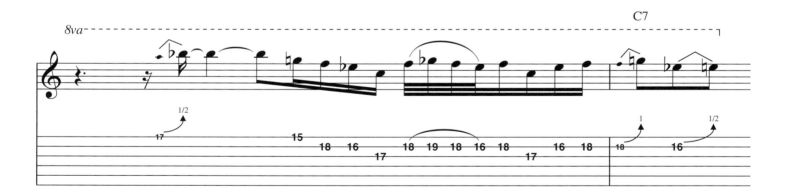

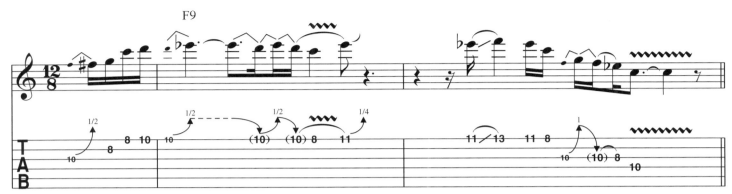

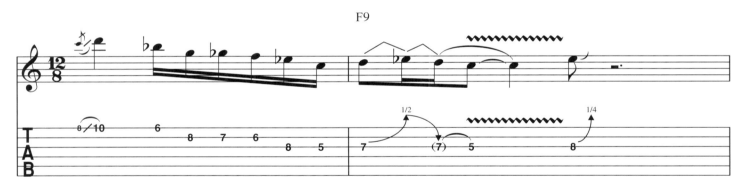

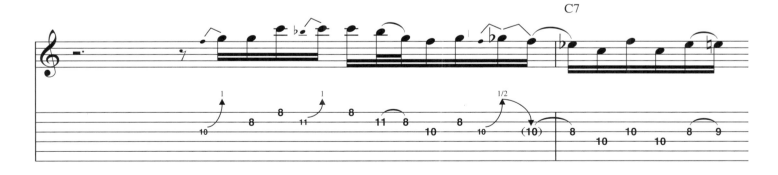

TRACK 45

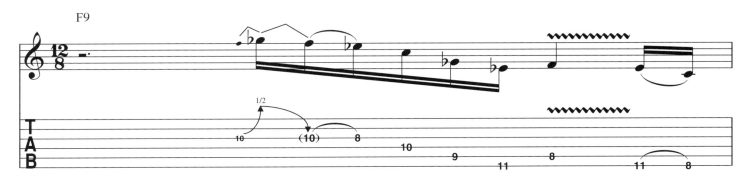

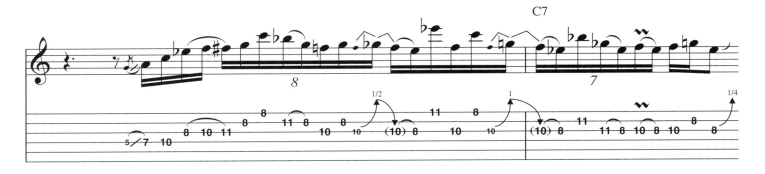

TRACK 46

*Played behind the beat.

Bars 7 and 8

The added descending chord sequence (C7–B7♯5–B♭13–A7♯9) in the following licks provides a harmonically lush background for Feiten to solo over but isn't really addressed specifically in the examples. Buzz simply keeps doing what he's been doing—creating authentic blues phrases without playing a new scale or mode over each of the dominant chords in the progression. The licks work so well in this context because they share many common tones with each altered chord. Take a closer look and you'll see just how cleverly they fit together. Buzz plays mostly with the C major pentatonic scale to take advantage of its many commonalities with the altered chords played by the band. Only in the third example does he hint at what is happening beneath him by playing the major thirds of each chord (E♭ over B7♯5, D over B♭13, and D♭ over A7♯9).

TRACK 47

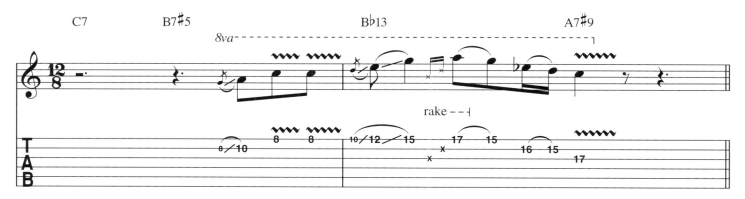

TRACK 48

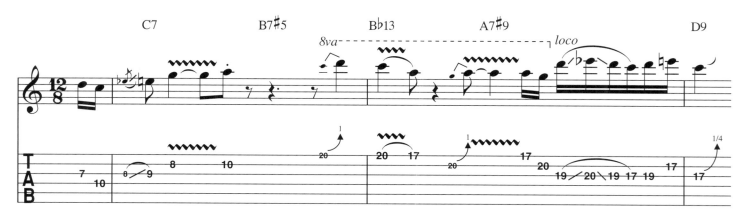

TRACK 49

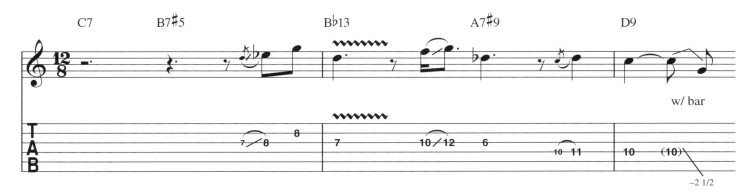

TRACK 50

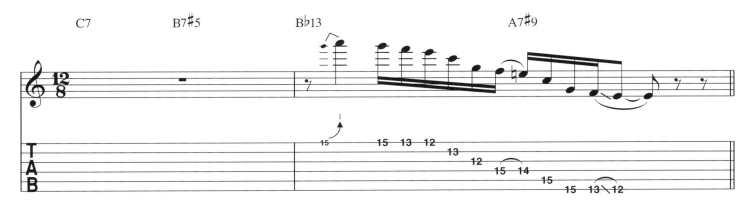

TRACK 51

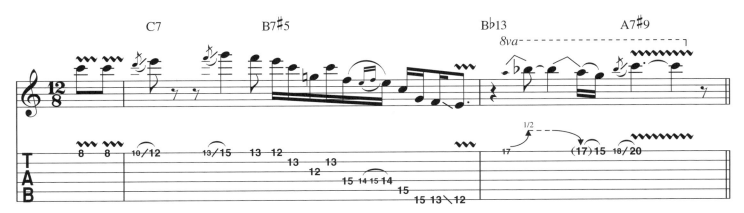

Bars 9 and 10

Buzz substitutes a II–V (D9–G7sus4) progression in this segment for the more familiar V–IV (G7–F7) progression but still uses the C major and minor pentatonic scales, often in combination, to create the following licks. Check out the many register jumps and tasty bends that keep things interesting. Also note the contrast between common tones that blend seamlessly with the underlying chords and the "clashing" (discordant) pitches, such as the E♭ found in the C minor pentatonic scale, that create a bit of tension when played over the D and G chords.

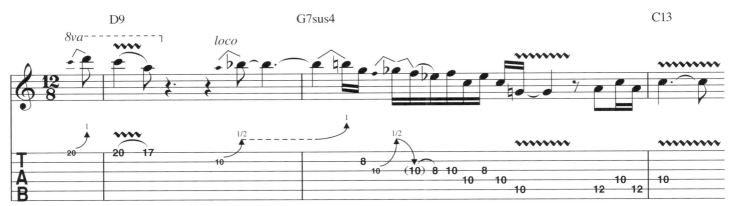

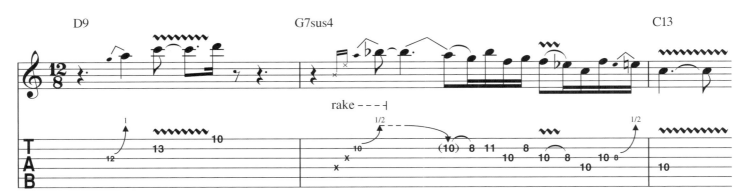

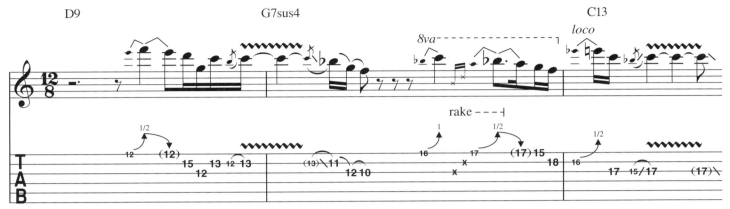

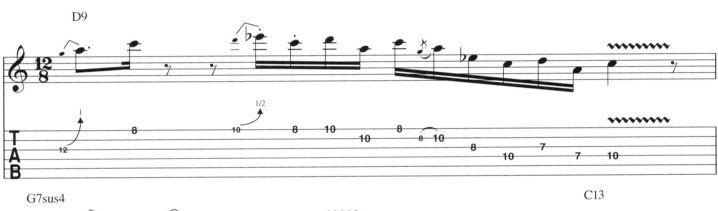

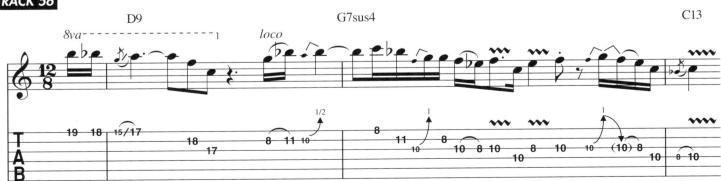

Bars 11 and 12

The final turnaround in our slow blues uses a I–VI–II–V (C13–A7#9–D9–G7sus4) progression that shows off a jazzy flair similar to what we heard in the earlier chord substitutions. Buzz keeps things firmly in the blues camp, however, by sticking mostly with major and minor pentatonic scales, rather than outlining each chord the way a jazz guitarist might. In fact, it is the very careful combination of these two scales that gives the licks such a satisfying blues flavor. Study them closely to see how they're combined—never haphazardly, but in a very specific, stylistically "correct" manner—and come up with a few of your own in the process. Remember that every musical genre has its own unique sense of grammar and diction, much like a spoken language, and notes (like words) are never merely thrown together. Instead, they flow in a logical sequence, accompanied by the appropriate punctuation (pauses and rests).

TRACK 57

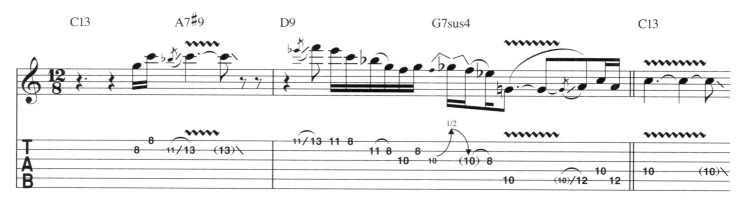

TRACK 58

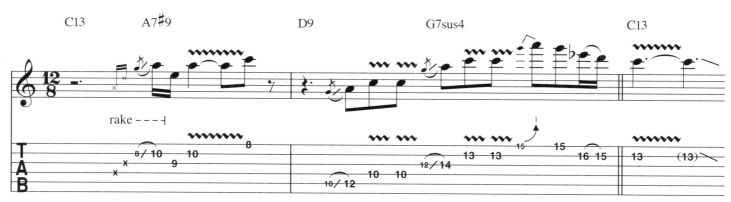

36

TRACK 59

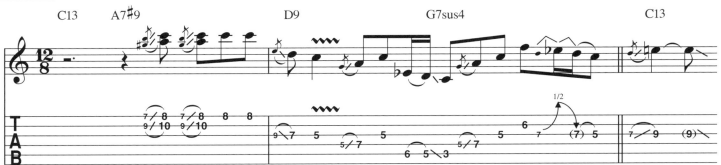

TRACK 60

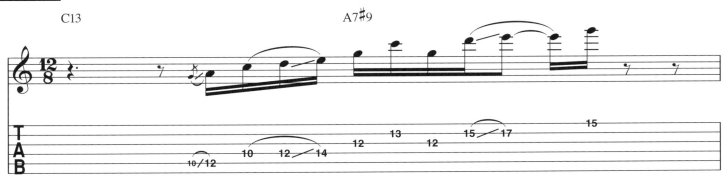

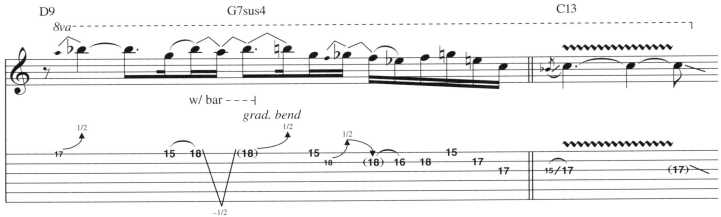

TRACK 61

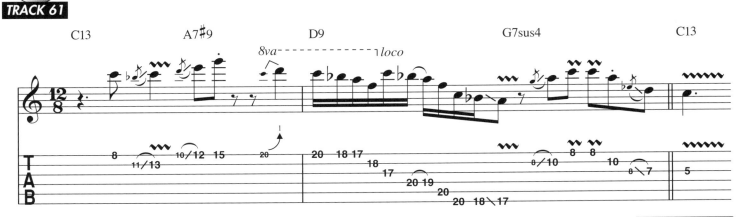

Fast Break Licks in E

Bars 1 and 2

"Stop-time" breaks in which the rhythm section drops out entirely or delivers a few carefully placed chordal "hits" can create interest and a sense of excitement for the audience and soloist alike. This focuses attention on the exposed soloist, giving him or her the chance to really shine. The licks below, in the key of E, work beautifully in such situations but also function well over standard grooves and rhythmic accompaniment as well. Both of the following licks are played at the top of the chorus and are taken from the E minor pentatonic scale. The first is played in the familiar 12th-position fingering while the second is in a higher register and begins with a ring finger bend on the high E string at the 17th fret.

TRACK 62

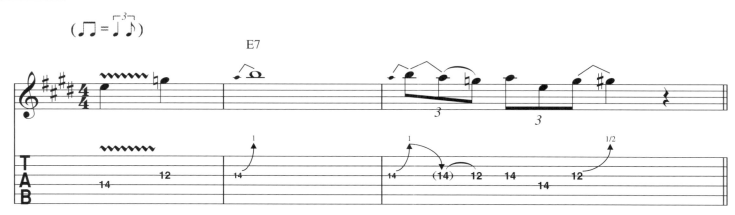

TRACK 63

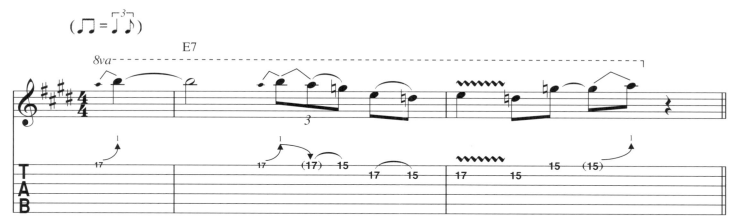

Bars 3 and 4

The next two licks are also played over the tonic (E7) but resolve upwards to the IV chord (A7) at their conclusion. Each features dramatic, sustained bends that push the 6th (C#) up to the flatted 7th (D) before being released and followed by a short minor-pentatonic phrase. Use your ring finger for each bend, and make sure to line up your middle and index fingers behind it to help push the string upwards.

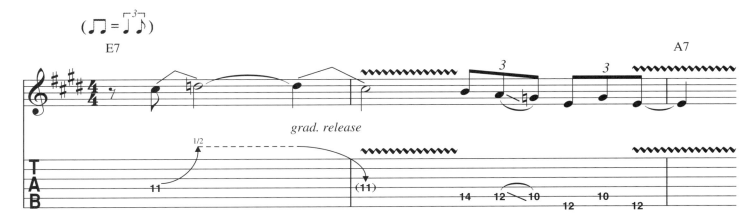

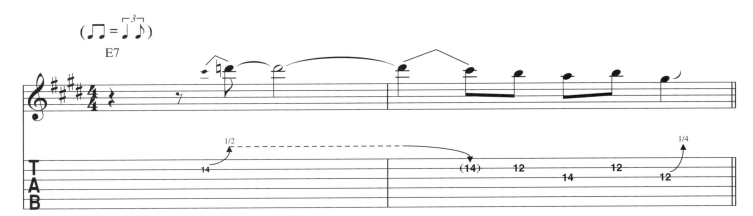

Bars 5 and 6

The next two licks are played over the IV chord (A7). The band may continue the stop-time hits in this section or return to playing "time" underneath the soloist here. The first lick is played in open position; use your ring finger for the B and high E string pull-offs and your middle finger for the bend, release, and pull-off on the G string. In the second lick, use your ring finger for the bend and release, and then pull off to your index finger at the 12th fret. Follow that up by playing the A at the 14th fret with your ring finger, then slide your index finger from the 12th fret to the 14th fret to match it.

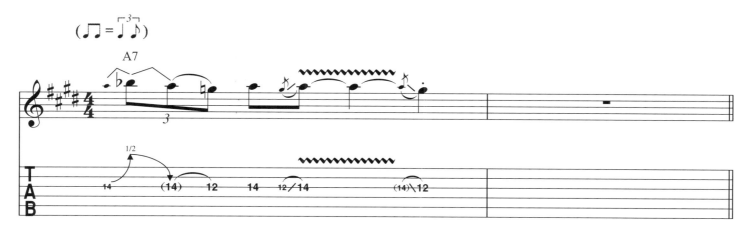

Bars 7 and 8

We move back to the tonic (E7) for the next two licks, biding our time before the big shift up to the V chord (B7) that's just around the corner. The first example is a simple "pitch-matching" phrase, in which we follow up a fifth-fret E on the B string by sliding into an E on the G string. The second lick is a bit more complex, featuring two pick rakes across the strings that end in targeted notes on the B and high E strings, as well as three distinctly different bends, and a few positional shifts.

TRACK 68

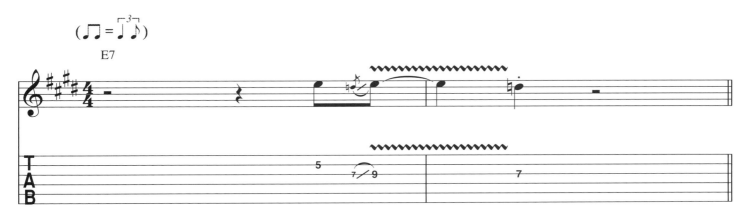

TRACK 69

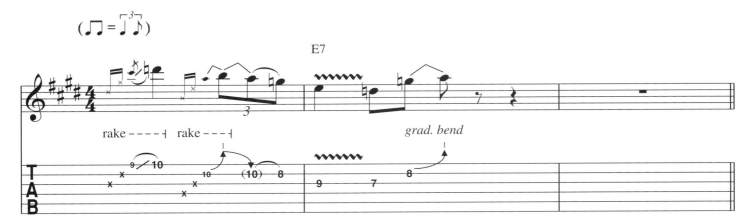

Bars 9 and 10

The following licks are played over the V–IV (B7 to A7) turnaround segment of the chorus. Each begins differently but ends with an identical move: the ring finger playing the E at the A string's 7th fret, followed by the index finger sliding into the same note from two frets below. In the first phrase, three separate rakes lead to ring-finger bends on the B string (twice) and the D string, while the second phrase features numerous position shifts and begins with an index-finger slide up the high E string from the 12th to the 14th fret. Use your ring finger for both bends in the second measure.

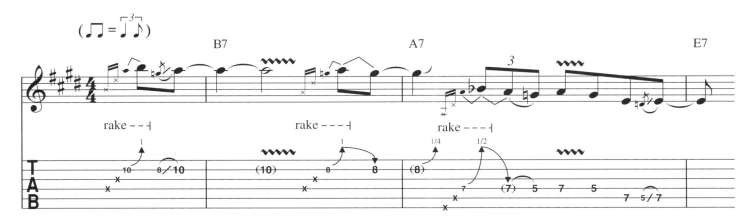

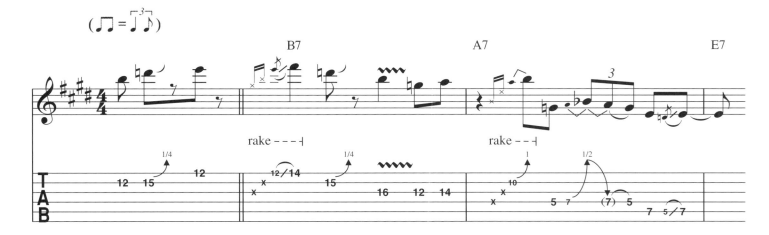

Bars 11 and 12

Our final two examples are played over the tonic (E7) but feature implied harmonic movement typical of a classic blues turnaround. Each requires a "hybrid" picking approach where you play the lower notes with the pick and pluck the upper notes with your middle finger. Both licks are a bit challenging, so work on them slowly and build them up to speed over time, paying particular attention to your fingering choices along the way. In the first phrase, use your middle and ring fingers on the D and B strings, respectively, in the first measure, then use an index-finger barre for the 7th fret notes in measure 2. In the second lick, use your index finger to play the descending notes on the G string while your middle finger frets the notes moving down the A string below.

Complete Solos

On Tracks 74–78 you can hear five of Buzz's complete uptempo solos in E. On Tracks 79–83 you can hear five of Buzz's complete slow solos in C. On Tracks 84–85 you can hear two of Buzz's complete stop-time solos in E.

      Full Uptempo Solos in E

      Full Slow Solos in C

   Full Stop-Time Solos in E

Jam Tracks

Now it's your turn to solo. Track 86 allows you to solo over an uptempo jam in E and Track 87 lets you solo over a slow jam in C.

  Uptempo Backing Track in E

  Slow Backing Track in C

Conclusion

This book is packed with material that will help any aspiring blues guitarist to enrich their soloing vocabulary, but a cursory reading and play-through will only hint at its vast potential. Instead of running quickly through the licks one after another, stop and consider the many ways each example could be used and re-interpreted. Pick a favorite phrase, then push, pull, and turn it inside out in as many directions as you can imagine. A single example could be the genesis of a world of musical possibilities. Transpose the lick to other keys and registers. Make it follow the chord progressions of the blues so that it moves up a 4th when the chords shift up a 4th. Push the lick through a variety of sequences within the scale from which it is built. Elongate or diminish the phrase rhythmically. Try displacing it rhythmically so that it begins and ends on a different beat than in its original form. Invert it so that it descends rather than rises, and vice-versa. These are just a few of the many ways a single, simple idea could be explored and exploited. There are no limits except those of your imagination.

The blues is a music of duality, happiness and pain, major and minor, technical prowess and emotional expression. It has one foot planted firmly in tradition while the other, by necessity, is pointed into the future, towards new generations of practitioners and new interpretations of decades-old material. One should never stop exploring and unearthing the work of the great bluesmen that created and perfected the style, but remember that we aren't creating a museum piece here; this is a living, growing art form that must always evolve if it is to remain as vital and expressive as it has been in the past.

GUITAR NOTATION LEGEND

Guitar music can be notated three different ways: on a *musical staff*, in *tablature*, and in *rhythm slashes*.

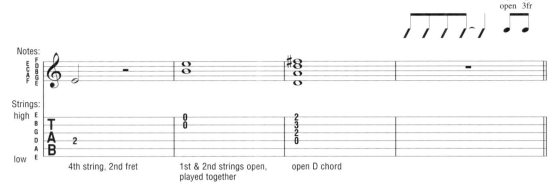

RHYTHM SLASHES are written above the staff. Strum chords in the rhythm indicated. Use the chord diagrams found at the top of the first page of the transcription for the appropriate chord voicings. Round noteheads indicate single notes.

THE MUSICAL STAFF shows pitches and rhythms and is divided by bar lines into measures. Pitches are named after the first seven letters of the alphabet.

TABLATURE graphically represents the guitar fingerboard. Each horizontal line represents a string, and each number represents a fret.

Notes:

Strings:
high
low

4th string, 2nd fret

1st & 2nd strings open, played together

open D chord

HALF-STEP BEND: Strike the note and bend up 1/2 step.

WHOLE-STEP BEND: Strike the note and bend up one step.

GRACE NOTE BEND: Strike the note and immediately bend up as indicated.

SLIGHT (MICROTONE) BEND: Strike the note and bend up 1/4 step.

BEND AND RELEASE: Strike the note and bend up as indicated, then release back to the original note. Only the first note is struck.

PRE-BEND: Bend the note as indicated, then strike it.

VIBRATO: The string is vibrated by rapidly bending and releasing the note with the fretting hand.

WIDE VIBRATO: The pitch is varied to a greater degree by vibrating with the fretting hand.

HAMMER-ON: Strike the first (lower) note with one finger, then sound the higher note (on the same string) with another finger by fretting it without picking.

PULL-OFF: Place both fingers on the notes to be sounded. Strike the first note and without picking, pull the finger off to sound the second (lower) note.

LEGATO SLIDE: Strike the first note and then slide the same fret-hand finger up or down to the second note. The second note is not struck.

SHIFT SLIDE: Same as legato slide, except the second note is struck.

TRILL: Very rapidly alternate between the notes indicated by continuously hammering on and pulling off.

TAPPING: Hammer ("tap") the fret indicated with the pick-hand index or middle finger and pull off to the note fretted by the fret hand.

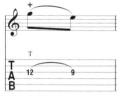

NATURAL HARMONIC: Strike the note while the fret-hand lightly touches the string directly over the fret indicated.

PINCH HARMONIC: The note is fretted normally and a harmonic is produced by adding the edge of the thumb or the tip of the index finger of the pick hand to the normal pick attack.

PICK SCRAPE: The edge of the pick is rubbed down (or up) the string, producing a scratchy sound.

MUFFLED STRINGS: A percussive sound is produced by laying the fret hand across the string(s) without depressing, and striking them with the pick hand.

PALM MUTING: The note is partially muted by the pick hand lightly touching the string(s) just before the bridge.

RAKE: Drag the pick across the strings indicated with a single motion.

TREMOLO PICKING: The note is picked as rapidly and continuously as possible.

VIBRATO BAR DIVE AND RETURN: The pitch of the note or chord is dropped a specified number of steps (in rhythm), then returned to the original pitch.

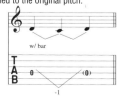

VIBRATO BAR SCOOP: Depress the bar just before striking the note, then quickly release the bar.

VIBRATO BAR DIP: Strike the note and then immediately drop a specified number of steps, then release back to the original pitch.

Great DVD selections from CHERRY LANE

Steven Adler's Getting Started with Rock Drumming
taught by the Legendary Former Guns N' Roses Drummer!
02501387 DVD $29.99

Altered Tunings and Techniques for Modern Metal Guitar
taught by Rick Plunkett
02501457 DVD $19.99

Beginning Blues Guitar
RHYTHM AND SOLOS
taught by Al Ek
02501325 DVD $19.99

Black Label Society
featuring Danny Gill
Guitar Legendary Licks
02500983 2-DVD Set $29.95

Black Sabbath
featuring Danny Gill
Guitar Legendary Licks
02500874 DVD $24.95

Blues Masters by the Bar
taught by Dave Celentano
02501146 DVD $24.99

Children of Bodom
ALEXI LAIHO'S LEGENDARY LICKS
taught by Danny Gill
02501398 DVD $24.99

John Denver
featuring Nate LaPointe
Guitar Legendary Licks
02500917 DVD $24.95

Learn to Play the Songs of Bob Dylan
taught by Nate LaPointe
Guitar Legendary Licks
02500918 DVD $24.95

Funky Rhythm Guitar
taught by Buzz Feiten
02501393 DVD $24.99

Grateful Dead – Classic Songs
featuring Nate LaPointe
Guitar Legendary Licks
02500968 DVD $24.95

Grateful Dead
featuring Nate LaPointe
Guitar Legendary Licks
02500551 DVD $24.95

Guitar Heroes
taught by Danny Gill
Guitar Legendary Licks
02501069 2-DVD Set $29.95

The Latin Funk Connection
02501417 DVD $19.99

Metallica – 1983-1988
featuring Doug Boduch
Bass Legendary Licks
02500481 DVD $24.95

Metallica – 1988-1997
featuring Doug Boduch
Bass Legendary Licks
02500484 DVD $24.95

Metallica – 1983-1988
featuring Nathan Kilen
Drum Legendary Licks
02500482 DVD $24.95

Metallica – 1988-1997
featuring Nathan Kilen
Drum Legendary Licks
02500485 DVD $24.95

Metallica – 1983-1988
featuring Doug Boduch
Guitar Legendary Licks
02500479 DVD $24.95

Metallica – 1988-1997
featuring Doug Boduch
Guitar Legendary Licks
02500480 DVD $24.99

Mastering the Modes for the Rock Guitarist
taught by Dave Celentano
02501449 DVD $19.99

Home Recording Magazine's 100 Recording Tips and Tricks
STRATEGIES AND SOLUTIONS FOR YOUR HOME STUDIO
02500509 DVD $19.95

Ozzy Osbourne – The Randy Rhoads Years
featuring Danny Gill
Guitar Legendary Licks
02501301 2-DVD Set $29.99

Pink Floyd – Learn the Songs from Dark Side of the Moon
by Nate LaPointe
Guitar Legendary Licks
02500919 DVD $24.95

Rock Harmonica
taught by Al Ek
02501475 DVD $19.99

Poncho Sanchez
featuring the Poncho Sanchez Latin Jazz Band
02500729 DVD $24.95

Joe Satriani
featuring Danny Gill
Guitar Legendary Licks Series
02500767 2-DVD Set $29.95

Joe Satriani – Classic Songs
featuring Danny Gill
Guitar Legendary Licks
02500913 2-DVD Set $29.95

Johnny Winter
taught by Al Ek
Guitar Legendary Licks
02501307 2-DVD Set 29.99

Johnny Winter
SLIDE GUITAR
featuring Johnny Winter with instruction by Al Ek
Guitar Legendary Licks
02501042 DVD $29.95

Wolfmother
featuring Danny Gill
02501062 DVD $24.95

See your local music retailer or contact

cherry lane
music company